Too Much Punch for Judy

for Judy

BY MARK WHEELLER

 ten alps communicate

Too Much Punch for Judy by Mark Wheeller

Sources:

"Judy" and her family; PC Abrahams; PC Caten; Essex County Council Highways Department; Essex Police; Sister Hunt; "Duncan" and The West Essex Gazette.

Author's acknowledgments:

All the sources for kind permission to use their words.
The performers in the Epping Youth Theatre productions QUENCHERS (1986) and TOO MUCH PUNCH FOR JUDY (1987):- Kim Baker; Fay Davies; Jo Dumelow; Paul Elliott; Nick Fradd; Ryan Gilbey; George Griffiths; Emma Jefferson; Garth Jennings; Debbie Mitchell; Debbie Pollard; Jo Redman; John Rowley; Barrie Sapsford; Beth Spendlow; Emma Turner; Anna Wallbank and John Ward.
Mick and Sylvia Baker for their initial inspiration and their tremendous support throughout the EYT performances. CADD (Campaign Against Drinking and Driving) for their tremendous campaign. Derek Rutherford, Institute of Alcohol Studies. David Lyndsay (then of Essex County Council Highways Department and, more recently, of North Yorkshire); his continuing support (even in the most difficult times!) is highly valued. Frank Nunneley (then of Hertfordshire County Council - Road Safety) and all the Road Safety Officers in England, Scotland and Wales who have offered their support to the play's continued success. Mat Kane, Antony Audenshaw and Yvonne Allen, and the **Ape Theatre Company** for their stunning performances since 1988 in England, Cyprus, Germany, Jersey. To Mat, Steve, Fay, and Tor for inspiring the "new" opening and closing scenes. Alistair Black, Hampshire County Council Drama Inspector, for the idea to re-visit the beginning of the play at the end... nice one! Meg Davis; Sophie Gorell Barnes and all at MBA Literary Agency for continued belief and support; Rachel Wheeller.

Too Much Punch for Judy received its professional premiere by **Touchstone Theatre In Education Company** in May 1987.

Too Much Punch for Judy was first published by the Institute of Alcohol Studies, 1988 (ISBN 1871195004)

This revised edition was published by **dbda** in 1999.
Reprinted July 2002, November 2003, March 2005 and July 2006.

ISBN 978 1 902843 05 6

BRITISH LIBRARY CATALOGUING IN PUBLICATION DATA
A catalogue record for this book is available from the British Library.

All enquiries regarding all rights associated with this play, including performing rights, should be addressed to: Sophie Gorell Barnes, MBA Literary Agents Limited, 62 Grafton Way, London W1P 5LD. Tel: 020 7387 2076   Fax: 020 7387 2042   E-mail: sophie@mbalit.co.uk

Further copies of this publication can be purchased from:
Ten Alps Communicate, 13th Floor, Portland House, Bressenden Place, London, SW1E 5BH.
Tel: 0845 303 3311   E-mail: hello@tenalpscommunicate.com

Introduction by Mark Wheeler

No-one is more surprised than me at the enormous success achieved (so quickly) by **Too Much Punch For Judy,** which I wrote initially as a 20 minute end section to a Youth Theatre play, **Quenchers,** about alcohol abuse. Since those initial performances in 1987, **Too Much Punch for Judy** has toured non-stop throughout schools, colleges, prisons, young offenders institutes and army bases. It has also been performed extensively in Australia, Cyprus, Eire, Germany, New Zealand and, most recently, Norway. In 1991, I was awarded the Prince Michael of Kent Special Award for Services to Road Safety Education for the play. **Too Much Punch For Judy** is now one of the most (if not the most) performed contemporary plays, with nearly 5000 performances between 1987 and 2003… all this from a 20 minute "extra" at the end of a production about alcohol misuse.

By the Christmas of 1985 the outline structure of our Youth Theatre play dealing with the dangers of alcohol was, we thought, complete. Then I saw the emotive (and very effective) Christmas drink/drive campaign. The subject of drinking and driving had not even crossed my mind… times were different then… drink/driving was something that everyone knew happened but few really thought seriously about it. Here was a real challenge for the play… to flag up a really important issue… and encourage an awareness of what was evidently a massive problem.

Soon after I spoke to our Schools Police Liaison Officer, I was put into contact with PC Chris Caten who, in turn, introduced me to "Judy".

Judy: *"Chris Caten explained that there was a local playwright looking for a story about drinking and driving. He wasn't at all sure that I'd want to do it but as he knew me quite well thought it was worth sounding me out. I thought… well… alright then, if someone's that interested I will… especially as Chris thought it was such a good idea. I didn't view the details of the accident as private… I'd made a dreadful mistake and… well… it didn't matter to me how many people knew… so long as it was going to do some good somewhere along the line."*

The local paper, the West Essex Gazette (who have always been supportive of the play), had been particularly sensitive in their coverage at the time of the accident, writing no more than a brief report. Consequently, the incident had not been "big" local news, so few actually knew "Judy's" story. There were even details of it, the research for this play uncovered, that "Judy" herself didn't know…

Introduction

she was for example completely unaware that anyone arrived on the scene prior to Chris Caten.

I met "Judy" on the 3rd January 1986. She was a wonderful 'subject' to interview; was incredibly open, making it easy for me to ask probing questions and, in describing events, quite naturally quoted lines of dialogue. I admired (and still do) her courage in coming forward. I left her house that day with the play planned out clearly in my head. It fell into place very naturally from that point on.

Judy: *"The main thing I remember about that first interview was getting upset at the point where I remembered I said 'Oh no... not my beautiful sister'. I remember having to stop at that point thinking I was going to start crying and feeling really stupid."*

From initial interviews I conducted with "Judy", her mum, Chris Caten, PC Abrahams, "Duncan" and Sister Davis, I was able to jig-saw together the first draft of the play.

I set myself the challenge of only using words spoken in the interviews to ensure that the play "rang true"... as true as joint memories would allow. Consequently the first draft was dense with monologues but it gave me a starting point to return to the relevant interviewees, to tease out more dialogue and check what had been selected for authenticity. Finally "Judy", Vi, Chris and myself had a meeting and went through each of the scenes where two or more of them appeared together. This was amazing. It ironed out any inconsistencies and also inspired new memories and therefore new words for the script.

Judy: *"If you're going to do an autobiographical play like this I think it's best to use the person's words to capture the way they speak, otherwise you can't begin to understand what sort of person they are. This wasn't a fairy tale to be messed around with... it's something that actually happened and, anyway, I don't think it would have had half the impact."*

One rehearsal, just a week before the premiere of **Quenchers**, illustrates how close this method of writing had come to getting the script 'right'. We were having great difficulty staging the section where Chris Caten reveals to Judy that Jo had died. The words were fine but should Chris be standing, kneeling beside her... how close should he be? I asked Chris to come in and add his comments. Chris watched but... his suggestions didn't seem to work. Then I asked Chris to do the scene... he didn't know the words.

Introduction

"No problem!" I retorted, "Just improvise."

Chris improvised and our "Judy" (Kim Baker) at that time, said the words from the script. Chris was able to show us how he broke the news... and with few exceptions he used the words we had in our script.

The approach was clearly, in my view, the right choice. Many who have seen the play say how powerful it is and comment on the authenticity of the words. The success and effectiveness of **Too Much Punch For Judy** stems from the fact that it is true and "Judy" is real. No attempt should be made in presenting the play to hide this fact, indeed by the use of slides, the "reality" can be drawn to the attention of the audience who need to disbelieve their suspension of disbelief. This Brechtian approach was the one used by the Playing Youth Theatre when they presented the first version of the play as the endpiece to "Quenchers" with the real "Judy" in the audience for the first time. It proved very successful.

Judy: "*I breezed through getting ready. I breezed into Harlow Playhouse, got into the Theatre and nearly lost control. I was flinching all the time and it made me sweat trying not to lose control. I didn't know whether to cry and walk out or be sick and walk out. I remember there were some young blokes, they were about eighteen... across from us, and they were crying. I was surprised... I never thought it would genuinely upset people like that, I really didn't.*"

Throughout the (long) run of **Quenchers** we picked up some tremendous reviews and also gained the interest and support of the Essex County Council Road Safety department. A very fruitful relationship quickly developed as they sponsored our performances at the Edinburgh Fringe Festival. Everyone had thought this would be a fitting end to this hugely successful project. I had other ideas... this was only the beginning!

I could see that the final section of **Quenchers** (sub-titled **Too Much Punch For Judy**, after a little known national Christmas Drink/Drive campaign) had enormous potential, as yet unrealised... but it had only told half the story. I began to realise that, rather than the night of the fatal accident appearing on its own, out of context, I should tell the story of Joanna and "Judy" from childhood. Fortunately, "Judy" was more than willing to co-operate, so I organised an interview which, like the others before, would be taped and painstakingly transcribed by hand.

Introduction

"Judy" talked openly about her childhood years and her relationship with Jo giving me plenty of material to work with. I combined these interviews with what her mother had said in her original interview and jig-sawed together a new opening section telling of "Judy's" early years and made a number of developments to the accident section.

Too Much Punch For Judy received its first public performance on Thursday 12th February 1987 in front of about forty people in the small Drama Studio at St. Johns School, Epping.

Judy: *"I thought that it was better than the extract in Quenchers, I thought it had more effect. It's not something I can enjoy, I switch off emotionally, otherwise I'd cry. When you're not ready for it, it does give you a bit of a wallop."*

The reviews following this performance were universally excellent.

Soon, Essex County Council were telling me that they wanted to sponsor a tour of the play. They would pay for the play to be performed in every school in Essex!!! I couldn't believe it! As it was unrealistic to release the Youth Theatre from their studies for eight weeks, a professional TIE company were hired... and the tour, much to my surprise, happened. The next thing I knew was that someone from Scotland had seen the play and they wanted it to tour Scottish schools. Since then it has toured across Britain almost continuously.

The next invitation was for the play to tour throughout Eire... then New Zealand!!! I was even invited out (paid for by the British Council... thanks!) to see the play and run some workshops. Amazing! It became the most performed play in New Zealand with John Godber's **Bouncers** coming in second! The most recent development has been the critically acclaimed TESTO performances in Norway.

Throughout this time, Ape have been touring the play non-stop throughout England; school/college Drama Departments have put on their own productions of the play and the ones that I have seen have been outstanding! It has won numerous One Act Play Festival awards.

As an examiner for GCSE drama I often read students' glowing reviews of Ape's performances. More recently I am being approached for permission to use extracts for A' level or audition speeches. To that end, I have adapted a monologue which will, I hope, prove useful to such students. All this from the smallest of small plays! It seemed that nothing could go wrong. But it did.

Late in the evening, shortly after the 5th October 1993, I received a phone call from Chris Caten. His tone immediately told me that something dreadful had happened. Nothing could prepare me for what he was about to say; "Judy" had been involved in a second drink/drive incident. Her car had collided with another and killed the 21-year-old driver immediately.

This tragedy defied belief. The emotional consequences for all involved, were more far reaching than I could ever imagine. The awful events (included in this version of the play) speak for themselves. A Road Safety Officer shocked me further by saying that, sadly, this incident supported statistics: Once you have been convicted of drinking and driving... you statistically are more likely to offend again than someone who has never done so! Do people never learn?

Clearly, there are no easy answers, but I sincerely hope that in continuing to promote this play we can all do our best to raise the issues and ensure that there are fewer tragedies around the corner. It is estimated that **Too Much Punch for Judy** has been seen by over half a million young people over the last ten or so years. The powerful tool of live theatre has been well served by the many versions of the play and the message of 'safe driving practices' communicated effectively and imaginatively by many theatre groups. How many lives have been saved? No one can answer that. Originally the aim of this play was to help put the problem of drinking and driving 'on the agenda'. I am certain that it has gone way beyond that.

This is a genuinely 'new' publication. In 2003 I went through all of the interviews and spotted parts that I missed firt time round. I made small alterations to the order of the 'jig-saw' and consciously made a point of stressing certain moments that were passed over. In this 25th anniversary version I have altered the beginning to place it in what is now much more obviously a historical context. I have also framed the main part of the play with a question that is, I think, pertinent to this type of theatre. I hope the availability of this new version of Too Much Punch For Judy will lead to new performances and new audiences and that the openly propagandist message is spelt out to even more people... young and old alike.

Don't drink and drive.

Good luck to all who choose to work with this play.

Props and Presentation

This play should be presented simply, yet imaginatively. Few props are required:

A wheelchair, two sets of car keys and two half-filled beer glasses.

Be imaginative with the other props... they can be much more symbolic: Empty beer crates (to sit on), a sheet (for the decorating scene / baby Leanne) and scaffolding poles for the accident scene.

For details of the accompanying book and DVD visit www.wheellerplays.com

List of Characters

5 male, 5 female, 3 male or female.

Judy:	A woman in her early 20s
Vi:	Judy's mother
Jo:	Judy's sister
Pete:	Judy's husband *(a non speaking part)*
Mark Wheeller:	Playwright
Rachael:	Mark's wife
Bob:	A cocky 'lad'
Nob:	Bob's sidekick
Voices/Actors:	Male or female
Duncan:	The first person on the scene of the accident
P.C. Caten:	Local Police Constable, friend of Judy's family
P.C. Abrahams:	Fresh, 'out of the box' Police Constable
Sister/Charge Nurse Davis:	Responsible for Judy in Hospital, male or female
Narrators 1 & 2:	Male or female

With doubling this play can be presented by 2 male, 2 female with parts allocated as follows:

Female 1:	Judy
Female 2:	Rachael; Vi; Jo; Narrator 1;
Male 1:	Bob; Voice; P.C. Caten *(taking P.C. Abrahams' lines)*; Narrator 2
Male 2:	Mark; Nob; Pete; Voice; Duncan; Charge Nurse Davis

Prologue

As written for the 25th Anniversary

Judy sits centrally on the stage. She is surrounded by people with scaffolding poles.

A simple representation of a car accident is presented accompanied by loud shouts of the following lines spoken simultaneously together with a single swing of the scaffolding bars.

All:	Judy, slow down a bit!
Judy:	Aaaaargh!
	(Silence)
Actor 1:	Between 1985 and 1987 Mark Wheeller wrote Too Much Punch For Judy.
Mark:	Judy felt this could be a way of bringing some good from her tragedy.
Actor 1:	Judy had killed her sister, Jo, in a drink drive incident in North Weald, where she lived.
Mark:	PC Chris Caten organised interviews for me. All the words in the script are those of the people involved.
Actor 1:	The play became a key part of international drink drive campaigns.
Mark:	Then, in 1993, (pace slows) the unbelievable happened.

A simple representation of a car accident is repeated again accompanied by loud shouts of the following lines spoken simultaneously together with the single swing of scaffolding bars.

All:	Judy, slow down a bit!
Judy:	Aaaaargh!
	(Silence)

Mark:	Judy was driving along the same stretch of road where she had crashed killing Jo ten years earlier. Only 200 metres from that accident Judy's car, on the wrong side of the road, hit another car killing the 21 year old driver Penny Jessup. Judy had been drinking and was twice over the legal limit. She also had traces of cannabis in her blood. Chris Caten phoned me late that evening:

(Mark and Chris are on the phone.)

PC Caten:	Oh and one other thing Mark. The press will want a quote. You should prepare something.
Mark:	OK. I will. Thanks Chris.

(They put down their phones. Caten exits.)

Rachael:	What was that all about?
Mark:	It was Chris Caten.
Rachael:	At this time of night? Is everything ok?
Mark:	Judy. She's been in another drink drive accident. A girl's been killed.
Rachael:	That's crazy!
Mark:	*(Nodding)* And it was on the same road as where she killed her sister.
	(Silence)
Rachael:	And she was over the limit?
Mark:	That's what Chris said.
Rachael:	Was she hurt?
Mark:	Apparently not. *(Pause)* And after everything she said.
Judy:	I will never drink and drive again as long as I live... never ever... I just couldn't do it.

Prologue

Mark: I am a very black and white kind of a person so thought talking to Judy would imply my support lay exclusively with her when my sympathies actually lay with the 21-year-old fatality in the second accident, Penny Jessup and her family. However, the situation regarding the future of the play, demanded I meet with Judy and…
I came to understand something my wife often said to me:

Rachael: Mark, not every situation is black and white.

Mark: When Judy answered the door she started to cry. (*She shows him to a seat.*) This was no moment to be judgemental.
Once we started talking I was reminded of how open she had been in those original interviews.

Judy: I can never pay for what I've done but I will at least be punished in prison. When I come out, I can try to start afresh. I haven't coped with problems in my life. Drink has numbed the pain and now it's led to this. I have voluntarily gone into counselling. I must replace drink with something else in my life.

Mark: (*Mark gets up to leave Judy's house.*) She was desperately unhappy.

(Judy stops Mark by saying)

Judy: Someone said I should write to her parents to say that I'm sorry. I'm not sure that will help. It goes beyond that doesn't it?

Rachael: How was she? (*Mark turns to Rachael as though they are mid conversation.*)

Mark: I couldn't cope if I were her.

Rachael: It must have been hard not to judge her.

Mark:	It wasn't actually. It was all a bit unreal. You know what? She is quite happy for the play to continue.
Rachael:	That's good isn't it?
Mark:	I'm not sure.
Rachael:	What do you mean?
Mark:	I wonder… am I kidding myself about all of this? If Judy hasn't learnt from her own mistakes, can the play ever have an effect on anyone?
Rachael:	I'd have to see it again, knowing what's happened, but I do think it can.
Mark:	So, let's have a look. Too Much Punch For Judy, pretty much as it was written in 1987.

All: January 1983:

Narrator 1:   Breakfast TV arrives in the UK.

(Loud vocal engine noises as Judy pushes Jo onto the stage in a wheelchair, very fast, as though they are messing around in a shopping trolley late at night.)

Jo: (*Screaming*) Judy! Judy! Slow down a bit!

Bob & Nob: Crash!

(Jo is tipped off the wheelchair, screaming, she falls to the floor on her back. The action freezes.)

Bob: Jo and Judy... sisters, out on the town.

Nob: ...with a shopping trolley from the local supermarket.

Judy: (*Back to life, laughing hysterically.*) Jo? Jo?

Jo: My back... Judy... my back.

Judy: What about your back? You're always on your back!!!

Jo: Cheeky tart! Something in my back's clicked.

Judy: Your having me on?

Jo: Course I am!

Judy: Bloody idiot! (*They laugh. Jo gets up.*)

Jo: Come on... or we'll be late for...

Judy & Jo: Aerobics...

All: February 1983.

Narrator 1:   Playwright Tennessee Williams dies in New York...

Narrator 2:   ... when he accidently swallows...

All: a plastic bottle cap!

Judy: At the gym.

Jo:	Losing weight...
Judy:	Till half past eight...
Jo & Judy:	Then... off to the Wine bar!
All:	March 1983.
Narrator 1:	CD's go on sale in the UK...
Narrator 2:	16 different albums from CBS records
Judy:	(*Adopting the voice of typical cookery TV personality.*) Today's new easy to follow recipe is "Smashed out of our Skulls" by Judy ...
Jo:	... and Jo
Jo & Judy:	Ingredients.
Jo:	Puerile conversation.
Judy:	Wine.
Jo:	Laughter.
Judy:	More Wine!
Jo:	Visit the Loo.
Judy:	And finally…
All:	More wine!
Judy:	Note:
Jo:	This recipe can be improved with a healthy portion of…
Jo & Judy:	Testosterone!
Jo, Judy, Bob & Nob:	Cue… Blokes in the Wine Bar!
All:	April 1983.
Narrator 1:	The one-pound coin is introduced in England and Wales.
Bob:	Bob...

Nob:	Nob!
Bob:	Looking good…
Nob:	… with slicked back hair.
Bob:	Feeling cool…
Bob & Nob:	No underwear!
Bob:	With throbbing – can't get enough of it - body tone.
Nob:	That's why they call us…
Bob & Nob:	"Testosterone"
Bob:	We are on the look out!
Nob:	Fishing line and hook out!
Bob:	Watering the nookey drought!
Bob & Nob:	Essex girls!!!
Nob:	Get 'em drinking.
Bob:	Stop 'em thinking.
Nob:	Give it some rabbit.
Bob & Nob:	In for the kill and grab it!
Jo & Judy:	Like two warriors they approach us…
Jo:	… that one's mine!
Judy:	"Good luck to you", I reply, as they trot out…
Jo & Judy:	… their crappy chat up line.
Bob:	Look at you two…
Bob & Nob:	… with your curves…
Nob:	… and us…
Bob & Nob:	… us with no brakes.
Jo:	Judy. What do you think?
Judy:	I think they're…

Jo & Judy:	...plonkers! (*They laugh hysterically.*)
Bob & Nob:	Do you wanna drink?
Judy & Jo:	(*Dead serious.*) Dry white wine... a bottle... each!
All:	May 1983:
Narrator:	Thatcher, wins a landslide General Election.
All 4:	Drink!
Bob:	Drink!
Judy:	Drink!
Nob:	Drink!
Jo:	Drink!

(*General merriment... perhaps a rowdy [rugby?] song.*)

(*The pace slows.*)

Narrator 1:	May 20th 1983:
Narrator 2:	A Friday.
Narrator 1:	The discovery of the retrovirus that causes AIDS is reported.
Judy:	Part two of our evening...
Bob:	A complete change of gear...
Nob:	Their good time drink...
Jo:	Calls death... to appear.
Vi:	And... in Epping...
Jo:	Jo...
Judy:	... and Judy...
Jo & Judy:	... drive home...
Vi:	Only 8 miles to Ongar...

(*The pace returns to that of Judy and Jo's lively night out.*)

Jo:	Come on Judy we'd better get out before we're thrown out.
Judy:	Wouldn't it be better if I drove?
Jo:	No; it's my car, it's my responsibility.
All:	(*Looking at Jo.*) Ignorance!
Judy:	I haven't had as much to drink as you. I'll only be a little over the limit.
All:	(*Looking at Judy.*) Ignorance!
Jo:	Ok then. (*She throws her car keys to Judy, who catches them.*) You drive. (*Silence*)

The mood changes suddenly. Judy remains motionless, looking at the keys.

Jo exits as Judy turns slowly... very slowly... to face the audience. The following lines are said with the obvious pain of the memory.

Judy:	It was just another night on the piss... but it wasn't... if anyone questioned it, everyone would just say...
Bob:	Them two?
Nob:	Don't worry about them.
Bob & Nob:	They're always pissed!
Judy:	You get so sure of yourself, so clever, well, not clever, you just don't think, 'cos you do it all the time.
	It only takes one person to point it out to you and you might not do it. Imagine if I see two people, drunk, who are going to drive home and I went over and told them what had happened to me last time I did it... they'd get a cab wouldn't they?

Judy: The accident happened on the 20th May 1983. Resigned... I think that's the word. I'm resigned to the fact that it has happened.
If you go through life with a big guilt complex afterwards, you just end up hurting everybody else as well as yourself, 'cos you get bitter and wound up. Nothing I can do is going to change it, ever. I wouldn't have harmed my sister, Joanna, not on purpose, so I don't feel guilty about killing her... because it was... an accident. I just know that I'll never be so out of control that I would put someone else's life in danger and I have never driven after drinking since.
Before it happens you think... "Oh, I won't get caught." I would probably never have got stopped and breathalysed. I'm having to pay for my mistake in a different way.

Vi: Tell you a bit about Joanna? *(Sigh)*
She was very extrovert, full of life, emotional... highly emotional, but a character. I mean, obviously to me she was beautiful, all your children are aren't they... but Jo was different. We were really good friends as well as mother and daughter. Even through my marriage break up Jo was very strong for me. Judy and Johnnie were both younger so it was always "Joey and the babies". It's so difficult to describe her... always willing, kind and thoughtful... an exceptional person.

Judy: Joanna was like my Mum's idol.
When I was young I felt a bit left out. I used to run away from home... to my Nan's... and take my hamster with me. She lived about a mile away, so I used to walk up there with my little hamster. I used to ask her not to let Mum know as she'd worry, but my Nan always rang her up.

Vi: To describe Jo or to put her into words is impossible. You had to know her... well she was just different. I don't think anyone ever said a bad word about her. Everyone said... "Oh, ain't your Jo a lovely girl!"

Judy: I was a bit of a bully, generally threatening people and frightening them, making them give me money and things, just horrible, really horrible. I didn't learn nothing at school. I liked English and Drama and got slung out of nearly all my others. My CSE cookery exam... that was a bit of a laugh. You have to make this meal, you know, starter, main course and afters. The starter: I can't remember what happened to that but the main course was Spaghetti Bolognese... well, in my case, just Bolognese 'cos I forgot to bring the spaghetti in!

For afters we had to make an apple pie. Mine sunk into the apple and, as if that wasn't bad enough, it then caught fire! You had to put it all on a table with your name on and everything. When the examiner came round she looked at mine and went *(feigning "posh" voice)* "Oh, deary, deary me! Just look at that one! Not very appetising, wouldn't you say?" and then she laughed!... Right out of order. So, I went up to her face, and I says: "Oy that's mine... and do you know what? I couldn't give a toss how 'appetising' you think it is 'cos I don't want to be a chef or nothing... you stupid old tart!" And I walked out saying... "I ain't fucking coming back to this dump no more!" And I didn't. I wasn't that bothered because I had a job at the hairdressers. A while later I got a letter saying to return any books I had that belonged to the school. *(She laughs)*... There obviously weren't any ... 'cos I didn't take none home.

Jo was always like the top ten in her class, really good, going to hockey matches and things. She'd come in from school, go into the dining room and spend hours on her homework, and me and Johnnie'd be out every night. She was really brainy. We didn't care for or like each other. She thought I was a ...

(Jo enters)

Jo & Judy:	Scruffy horrible little idiot.
Judy:	She always put me down for...
Jo & Judy:	... wearing jeans, being scruffy and not bothering to look good.
Judy:	I remember one time when we were all talking about what we were going to wear to a wedding reception...
Jo:	And what are you going to wear? Jeans?
Judy:	Yeh, probably will!
Jo:	How can you wear jeans to a wedding?
Judy:	I don't give a toss! If they don't like it they can sling me out! I'll wear what I want to wear!

(Silence. Pete enters and presents Judy with a "baby"... don't use a doll, a folded sheet is much more flexible and can be re-used in a different way in the following scene.)

Judy:	I got married when I was seventeen. Joanna was always out and about every night while I was the old frumpish housewife. When I split up with the man I was married to... *(the man exits leaving Judy with the "baby")*... I started going round with Jo 'cos she was working in Epping... but I still couldn't go out a lot 'cos I had my baby... Leanne.

(Judy puts the "baby" down... to sleep. Jo enters... in a cameo scene they have "fun" punctuated by downing drink.)

Vi:	Joanna was an absolute brick to Judy during that time. She'd take her out and help her with Leanne. She was absolutely brilliant.
Judy:	Jo didn't have a boyfriend so she used to come round and stay with me. We was always laughing ... everything would just crack you up... you'd think everything was funny. One night... we'd been to see the New Vaudeville Band... you know... *(singing)* "Winchester Cathedral"... not that we thought they were cool, but Jo knew one of the blokes.

	Anyway we got to the traffic lights near the Indian restaurant in Epping and pulled down this entrance... I don't remember why. Anyway, we got stuck in loads of mud so Jo got out and pushed the car.
Jo:	When I say rev it up... rev it up!
Judy:	She was giving it an almighty push and I revved it up. She came round to me, and tapped on my window, deadly serious, I'll never forget, and said...
Jo:	You fucking idiot!
Judy:	When I turned round I saw she was completely pebble dashed in mud! She was really dressed up in this beautiful suede jacket. Well, we were just in hysterics for about ten minutes before we could get the car out.

(They both laugh... sharing the memory.)

Judy:	When most people go out, they have a few drinks, have a nice evening out. We used to go out... and go mental. Jo could out-drink any bloke... whereas me... I'd have three glasses of wine and I'd be in a terrible state!

(They both laugh loudly... followed by a sudden silence. Turning slowly to the audience.)

Judy:	We was always out drinking. That's all we ever did ... go out and go wild. I'll tell you something that is really weird. It was really strange. We were in her new flat doing some decorating and she said:
Jo:	I think I'll make a will.
Judy:	Joanna! You think of the most funny things! What on earth do you want to make a will for?
Jo:	I just feel that I should. I mean if anything happens to me now I've got the flat, there could be quite a bit of money involved... and I'd want your Leanne to have it.

Judy:	What? You can't be serious.
Jo:	Well, you don't know this... but Denise did my Tarot cards... twice... and I got the death one... both times.
Judy:	Joanna! You shouldn't mess around with things like that. I'd never go into Denise's house... let alone do that! it's like the Evil Dead house... really creepy!
Jo:	Don't be stupid! What can happen to you?
Judy:	If I pulled it out, that'd be it! I'd be so frightened I'd be like the Doomsday book, walking around, wondering when it's going to happen.
Jo:	You're being silly! Denise told me it doesn't necessarily mean that you, personally are going to die; it could mean the death of a relationship.
Judy:	Aren't you scared?
Jo:	No. Why? Should I be? *(Silence)*
Judy:	One week later we had the accident. *(Pause)* The Monday before the accident I gets this phone call from Jo. *(Yawning)* It was about five or six o'clock in the morning...
Jo:	It's me.
Judy:	What the hell do you want?
Jo:	Can you come and pick me up?
Judy:	Where are you?
Jo:	Saffron Walden police station.
Judy:	What 've you done?
Jo:	Got stopped for drinking and driving and they won't let me drive my car home 'cos I'm still over the limit and I've got to get to work.

Judy: Ok. I'll come and get you. Stay where you are.
I went over there, took her to work and took her back to get her car in the evening. She didn't seem too bothered about it really.
What on earth are you going to do? How are you going to get to work if you're banned?

Jo: I dunno. I'll have to think of a way round it when I've been to court.

Judy: Well, there's not a lot of transport from Dunmow to Epping, is there?

Jo: Don't worry! Alison goes into Epping at about the same time, she'll give me a lift. I'll get round it somehow... it's not your problem so don't worry!

Judy: How much had you had to drink?

Jo: Just the usual.

Judy: Yeh?

Jo: ... some wine... not a lot.

Judy: Don't you see! You'll be banned! I bet you were well over the limit!

Jo: Judy! You're more worried about it than I am! Look! I don't want anyone else to know. I want you to promise me you won't tell Mum. *(Pause)* You know what she's like; it'll make her worry and it's not necessary.

Judy: Ok then.

Jo: I want you to promise.

Judy: I won't tell Mum... I promise.
(They freeze. Silence)

Vi: The day of the accident Joanna phoned me and said...

Jo: Are you coming into lunch today Mum? Terry and Trisha are coming... so why don't you come too?

Vi: So I did. We had a right old laugh, as you can imagine. Then we went back to her office, so that she could do some work and, like we was all in a laughing mood.
I left there about a quarter past five and she said she was meeting Judy...

Jo: She's coming to aerobics... I said if she came I'd take her to the wine bar after.

Vi: Well, be careful in the car If you're drinking, it may be best for you to stay at Judy's. It'd be stupid to travel all the way back to Dunmow.

Jo: Mum!

Vi: Just be careful!

Jo: Mum! You worry when I go to the lav!

Vi: "Yeh! I do!" *(Silence)*

They were the last words I said to her
Then I went home. *(They embrace. Vi exits.)*

Judy:	We'd been to the Epping Sports Centre doing an aerobics class, and after a couple of drinks there we went on to the Wine bar. It was only around the corner so we walked. I wasn't drinking as much as Jo; I hadn't had an enormous amount; I should imagine about three quarters of a bottle of wine which to me isn't a lot of drink. I certainly didn't **feel** drunk. Jo had drunk an awful lot so I suggested that it would be better if I drove:
Jo:	No! It's my car. It's my responsibility.
Judy:	Jo, what's going to happen if you do get pulled up? You'll go to court with two drink drive convictions which means a huge ban and a ridiculous fine!
Jo:	No, it's my car!
Judy:	Look, I haven't had as much to drink as you, so I'm only going to be a bit over the limit and anyway, even if I did get caught, it makes no odds 'cos I don't need to drive as much as you what with your job and...
Jo:	Ok then. You drive.

(Jo throws the car keys to Judy. They freeze the moment as Judy catches the keys. Silence.)

Judy:	We got into the car with me in the driving seat and put a tape on.

(WE'VE ONLY JUST BEGUN⁽¹⁾ by the Carpenters fades in slowly and underpins the duration of the accident scene.)

Judy:	It's only about five miles from the Epping Sports centre to North Weald where I live. The last thing I remember is driving past the hospital.
P.C. Caten:	I was out with a fairly young PC. We'd been static at Scratch Bridge in North Weald for about half an hour.

(1) The performing rights for this play do not cover the right to use this or other pieces of pre-recorded music. Permission will be required from the appropriate bodies.

P.C. Abrahams:	As far as I can remember, it was about five to twelve and we'd decided to go in at midnight to have a cup of tea.
P.C. Caten:	As we made our way towards Epping, I happened to note Jo and Judy drive by. I'd known their family for... well over ten years. I supposed they'd been out enjoying themselves.
Judy:	I was used to driving a bigger car with powered steering and I guess what must have happened is that where I was a bit drunk I forgot I was in Jo's car and just didn't turn the wheel enough on this bend at Scratch Bridge. I can't remember going off the road, I can't remember hitting the kerb or anything. God, it must have took off when we hit that kerb. Every now and then I get flashbacks, I keep thinking that she told me to slow down, but I can't remember her being in the car. I can't really remember anything.

(The following speeches are made simultaneously)

Actor 1: Ok then; you drive.

Actor 2: No it's my car it's my responsibility.

Actor 1: I think I'll make a will.

Actor 2: I'm only going to be a bit over the limit.

Actor 1: Them two. They're always pissed they'll be alright.

Actor 2: I got the death card both times.

Actor 1: Today's easy to follow recipe "Smashed out of our Skulls".

Actor 1 & 2: Ok then. You drive.

Judy: Wouldn't it be better if I drove? What's going to happen if you do get pulled up? You'll go to court with two drink drive convictions which means a huge ban and a ridiculous fine!

I haven't had as much to drink as you, so I'm only going to be a bit over the limit and anyway, even if I did get caught, it makes no odds. I don't need to drive as much as you what with your job and...

Jo: Judy! Slow down a bit!

The accident is simulated stylistically somehow!!! It has been presented in a variety of ways. I would suggest the use of scaffolding bars and loud screams... attempting to capture the essence of the accident... speed... impact... fright... whiplash... the sound of metal on metal... and finally silence and stillness.

Duncan: I guess it was about midnight and there was one hell of a mighty crash, completely and utterly unannounced by any of the normal sounds that one might associate with a road accident... howls of tyres, screeching and what have you. I was just mesmerised. I couldn't think what it was and all I could hear was "We've Only Just Begun" by the Carpenters blasting out from what I later discovered to be the car stereo. I got out of bed and looked out of the window.

SLIDE 1(2)

Duncan.   There was a Renault 5 buried in the bridge, just literally sort of disappeared into the bridge parapet. My immediate reaction was "Oh shit! I don't want to be involved in that! I'll let someone else go and have a look." I waited... maybe half a minute, hoping that someone would get out of the bloody thing... but nobody did. In the end, I pulled on a pair of trousers, a pullover but stupidly nothing else and shot across there.
I couldn't approach the car from the passenger side it was too badly damaged so went to the driver's door. It wouldn't open. I looked inside. I could see two shapes. I tried the door again. The music was blasting out, like it was sort of force ten on the decibel scale.
At that point I suddenly realised that I was standing around in bare feet with a lot of glass about the place which was pretty bloody stupid. I thought...
"well, nobody else is coming out to help!", so I shot back inside, dialled 999, reported the accident... oh yes ... and put some shoes on!

(2) Slides, police photos of the accident to be shown in this scene are available from
www.wheellerplays.com where you will also find details of the accompanying book and DVD.

P.C. Abrahams: We'd only gone about half a mile further, towards the police station, when our information room called up.

Voice: *(FX over radio.)* Any unit to attend a serious RTA in North Weald.

SLIDE 2

P.C. Abrahams: We can attend. We're in North Weald. Can you give us an exact location?

Voice: *(FX over radio.)* The informant is telephoning from Harrison Drive. The accident was on Scratch Bridge.

P.C. Abrahams: We'll attend. E.T.A. one minute.

Duncan: I went back to the car which was now smelling of petrol, battery fluid, anti freeze and there was this dripping and hissing. I was afraid it might catch fire so, put my leg up onto the back wing and forced the driver's side door open.
The music was still blasting out, so the first thing I did was to turn off the power which produced dead silence.
I was then confronted with these two forms and a strong smell of alcohol. I remember that clearly, the smell of alcohol and... well, cheap perfume.
I felt for a pulse on the passenger. I couldn't find one. There were no... no life signs at all. *(Pause)*

SLIDE 3

Duncan: The bridge they'd hit was just these upright concrete pillars with scaffolding pipes coming through them. One of these pipes had been bent, come straight in, through the windscreen, missed the driver... but it was such that the passenger had to have been hit by it. Her head was in a position where it had obviously been thrown back by the force of this pole coming in directly on... to her face. I was sufficiently squeamish not to investigate that one any further. Thank Christ it wasn't bloody daylight, that's all I can say.

I remember thinking... "the passenger is either dead or alive. If she's dead, well I can't do anything about it, but what if she starts to wake up, with hideous bloody injuries requiring some attention, what the bloody hell am I to do then?" I've done my bit of first aid, but this was way, way, way beyond that.,, or anything I'd experienced in my life.

That's the frightening thing about it. The fact that she was dead... was a bloody blessing!

(He goes to Judy.)

By this time the driver had begun to make signs of recovery, so I managed to find the buckles of her seat belt and release her.
"Right, lets get you out of here."
She was like a sort of bendy toy really... I soon realised that she was smashed out of her skull... drunk.

Judy: What on earth happened down there?

Duncan: I'm afraid you've had a bit of an accident dear. Can you tell me what your name is?

Judy: Judy. *(Pause)*
There was glass in the car. I remember glass and blood on the floor of the car; where did it all come from?

Duncan: We'll find out later.

Judy: Where's my handbag? I want my handbag! It must be in the car!

Duncan: No, you hang on here a minute love.

Judy:	My sister! I've got to get to Joanna! She's still in the car! Don't you bloody touch me! I want to go and see if she's alright!
Duncan:	No! We'd better wait here. I've phoned the police, so they'll be here in a minute.
Judy:	What's wrong with Joanna? Fucking let go of me! *(She crumples. Resigned.)* Why won't you let me go back to the car?
Duncan:	I thought she was going to get so hysterical that I just wouldn't be able to cope, but she didn't actually; she just seemed to go limpish and start to cry. At that point the police car came down the road like a bat out of hell! I don't think that it had stopped before the doors were opened and a young PC ran out towards us. There's someone else in the car.
P.C. Abrahams:	I'll go down.
Duncan:	He went down to the passenger side of the vehicle and shone a torch in there. Obviously he was having difficulty seeing inside because he kept angling his head.
P.C. Caten:	It's Jo Poulton. I can't believe it! Jo and Judy.
P.C. Abrahams:	Do you know them then?
P.C. Caten:	Yeh. I can't get a pulse at all!
P.C. Abrahams:	Look! Smoke under the bonnet.
P.C. Caten:	You go and get the extinguisher... I'll phone HQ and then go and see the driver... she's Jo's sister. *(Abrahams exits. P.C. Caten speaking to radio.)* Golf -golf -two -one. Regarding RTA that we are attending in North Weald. We require immediate back up. Possible fatal. Will require two ambulances. I repeat **two** ambulances.

Duncan:	I can remember holding this woman, listening to him report back and nodding as he said "fatal". She didn't hear anything. I'm absolutely positive that she had no idea at all... though she must have surely suspected something.
P.C. Caten:	Thanks for your help. It's good of you to come out.
Duncan:	Is it OK for me to go back home now?
P.C. Caten:	Yeh. I know Judy... don't I love.., so I'll make sure that she's OK. Thanks again for coming out.
Duncan:	I live over there. If you want any further information ... feel free to know...

I went back home and poured myself a great big bloody drink! I opened the curtains and stood and watched the proceedings... just out of morbid curiosity... I'm afraid that's inherent in all of us in those kinds of circumstances.

I remember feeling slightly angry that so many houses that faced onto it had obviously decided that they didn't want to become involved... it's just a silly sort of reaction you get in a state of stress... 'cos I do understand why... but bloody muggins here... why did I have to go out and get involved?

I didn't sleep at all. The realisation that you've come right next to an extremely violent death was a very unnerving and shattering experience... and it was annoying. This bloody woman who drove this bloody car hadn't even touched the brakes... well she couldn't have done! There wasn't a mark on the road anywhere! She was that drunk!

She didn't even know that she'd gone up the kerb, along the pavement and into the bridge parapet... she was that drunk!

P.C. Caten:	My main job now was to keep Judy away from the accident and her mind off Jo. She had glass in her hair, blood on her fingers, was very disorientated and continued to cry. I carried her to the police car and spoke to her to reassure her that everything that could be done was being done. Eventually the ambulance arrived. "Judy, where's your daughter? Where's Leanne?"
Judy:	She's at home. I've got a baby-sitter. What'll happen?
P.C. Caten:	It's Ok. I'll sort something out whilst you're being taken to hospital.
Judy:	What about Joanna? Isn't she coming?
P.C. Caten:	They're just getting her out. She'll be coming in another ambulance.
Judy:	Why can't she come in this one?
P.C. Caten:	I'm afraid that she's a bit more hurt than you are.
Judy:	Why can't we wait? I want her to come with me!
P.C. Caten:	No! We need another ambulance for her.
Judy:	I remember turning round as they put me in the ambulance and seeing the car hooked on the railings up in the air. I didn't see the front of the car at all. They kept me round my side of the car which was alright. It weren't smashed or nothing... It was all up in the air and like tipping forward and the wheels were off the ground and I thought... "Oh look at that!!" I didn't think that Jo had been really injured... it didn't even enter my mind that she could have been killed.
P.C. Abrahams:	After they'd got the passenger out of the car I had to keep members of the public who'd come out to watch away from the scene as it wasn't a particularly pretty sight. When they started to get her out of the car they realised that she had quite severe injuries so they had to... somebody got some black plastic bags which they put over her head and shoulders... just to make it a little bit better for people that were gathered around.

P.C. Caten:	We made our way to her mother's house. We had to break the news to her. I will admit that I was controlling my feelings more than I've ever had to before. I took a deep breath and knocked on the door.
P.C. Abrahams:	There was no reply. We tried several times again.
P.C. Caten:	That's strange. Judy said she'd be in.
P.C. Abrahams:	No one answered so we came away.
Duncan:	*(As this speech is portrayed any "debris" from the accident can be cleared up.)* I've recently been reading THE SHOOTING OF PRESIDENT KENNEDY. He was apparently lying in the hospital after he died and the hospital was returning to normal. There was a comment made, that next door, two janitors... auxiliaries were laughing... laughing over a joke. There was this hollow laughter going down the corridor with a dead president there... a very harsh irony eh? Well, a similar thing happened in this situation. The ambulance had gone, and you were left with the "roadies" trying to drag the car off the bridge parapet. They were laughing and I thought... that can't be right. My final reaction was the following morning. I went out there and "society" had cleared up the mess. "Society" had come along with its back up force and cleaned up the mess... you know... the ambulance had taken away the broken body... and the mortuary had taken care of it from then on. There wasn't any blood... there wasn't anything. The place had been sanitised. It was an extraordinary sensation, and yet a human life had disappeared there, and you felt... well I felt that there should be something there that actually proved the point... but there was nothing.

Vi:	I woke up. I heard a rat-a-tat-tat at the door. I looked out of the window and saw a police car drive away and... oh... it's a sick feeling. Know what I mean? I thought... something's happened to Johnnie... he's been nicked or something... so I came downstairs and rang Ongar police station. I couldn't get a reply so I rang Epping.
Voice:	Everything's alright Mrs. Poulton. They were just trying to get in touch. I'll let them know you're there.
Vi:	I made a cup of coffee and sat down... and... oh your mind is going. They were very nice... but... you know... there's something inside you; you think: something's up. Ten minutes later they were back.
P.C. Caten:	Hello Vi.
Vi:	Chris! What is it? Is it Johnnie? It's Johnnie isn't it? *(Pause)* Has something happened... do you want to come in?
P.C. Caten:	Yes. Look I think you'd better sit down. I've got some very bad news for you.
Vi:	It's Johnnie... I know what it's about. You know me ... I can take anything.
P.C. Caten:	Vi... it's not to do with John at all.

(The following speeches are made simultaneously)

Vi:	It's Jo. *(Silence)* What's happened to her?	Judy:	*(Enters)* Wouldn't it be better if I drove.
		Jo:	*(Enters)* No. It's my car. It's my responsibility.
P.C. Caten:	Please sit down.		

Judy:	I haven't had as much to drink as you. I'll only be a bit over the limit.
Jo:	Judy! Slow down a bit! *(Judy screams and moves into a freeze reminiscent of the crash.)*

Actors 1 & 2, Duncan:	Joanna, just be careful in the car. If you're drinking it may be best for you to stay at Judy's; it'd be stupid to travel all the way to Dunmow. Just be careful.
P.C. Caten:	Joanna's been killed in a road accident.

*Fade up appropriate music prior to the commencement of the
following speeches – made simultaneously. As the speeches begin,
Jo and Judy break out of their freeze and laugh hysterically, a
dreamlike quotation from the scene where the car was stuck in the
mud... a nightmarish memory of the happy sisters playing in Vi's
mind. Throughout this hysterical laughter they look at Vi. They stop
laughing as they see Vi become faint.*

P.C. Caten:	Actors 1 & 2:	Duncan:
Vi. Listen. She didn't suffer. It was very quick. Vi... do you understand what I'm saying...? *(Vi finds it difficult to take in and becomes lost in her memories.)*	Then we went back to the office so she could do some work and... like... we was all in a laughing mood. I left there at about a quarter past five and she said: "Judy's coming to aerobics... I said if she came I'd take her to the wine bar after."	This bloody woman who drove this bloody car hadn't even touched the brakes... well she couldn't have done! There wasn't a mark on the road anywhere! She was that drunk. She didn't even know that she'd gone up the kerb, along the pavement and into the bridge parapet... she was that drunk!

*(Song fades – all exit except P.C. Caten and Vi.
P.C. Caten gently comforts Vi and encourages her to sit.)*

P.C. Caten:	She was a lovely girl. I've come here tonight because I thought it would help you to have someone you know breaking the news to you. You have got to pull yourself together and be very brave. Judy was involved as well. She's in hospital now, and she needs you.

Vi:	Does she know about Joanna?
P.C. Caten:	No they're waiting...
Vi:	Are you sure she's alright?
P.C. Caten:	She's in shock, but I don't think she has any serious injuries. They've taken her to St. Margaret's Hospital. *(Silence)*
Vi:	Was it Jo's car?
P.C. Caten:	Yes... but... but Judy was driving.
Vi:	But Jo never let anyone drive her car... Chris are you sure?
P.C. Caten:	Yes, certain.
Vi:	But I don't understand... why would Judy be?... it doesn't make sense. Will I have to identify her?
P.C. Caten:	I've already done it.
Vi:	Do I have to see her?
P.C. Caten:	No. No you don't. *(Silence)*
Vi:	Do you think I ought to go to St. Margaret's to see Judy?
P.C. Caten:	I think it's very important that you speak to her.
Vi:	No way did I want to know what had happened. I just wanted to remember Jo as she was when I walked out of the office. No way did I want to know. All I knew was that my Joanna was dead. Chris said that it was instantaneous. It's strange, but, a few years before, I'd had a really nasty road accident, and I didn't remember a thing until I came round in the ambulance and then it was... oh, I hurt like hell. Well, Joanna never came round... and that's how I know she didn't suffer. So that experience has eased my mind about her last moments.

(Vi cries/sobs. She is alone for some moments as appropriate pre-recorded music swells. P.C. Caten leads Vi out slowly. Jo and Judy enter from either side of the stage and direct their lines to the other. They build gradually to a climax... as though it is a row and perhaps again move into freeze motifs reminiscent of the accident.)

Jo:	It's my car. It's my responsibility.
Judy:	Jo, what's going to happen if you do get pulled up? You'll go to court with two drink drive convictions which means a huge ban and a ridiculous fine!
Jo:	No, it's my car!
Judy:	Look, I haven't had as much to drink as you, so I'm only going to be a bit over the limit and anyway, even if I did get caught, it makes no odds 'cos I don't need to drive as much as you what with your job and...
Jo:	Ok then. You drive. *(Exits)*
	(Silence)
Sister/Charge Nurse Davis:	*(Enter Sister/Charge Nurse Davis with a wheelchair. Jo exits. Davis gets Judy to sit in the wheelchair.)* When the driver was brought in I was told that she had no obvious injuries, but was very shocked. The ambulance crew were absolutely shattered by the accident... it was horrific... they were devastated by the state of Judy's sister. I was told that she was being taken straight to the mortuary. We felt that it was in Judy's best interests to delay telling her about her sister until she had some family support. I went over to her to take her through to Casualty.
Judy:	*(Referring to the wheelchair.)* I don't need this! I ain't a bleedin' cripple!
Davis:	You can't walk on your own just yet.
Judy:	Well, I don't want this fucking blanket.

Davis:	You'll have to. You're in shock and you might catch a chill. She was shaking, crying, a bit hysterical, typical road accident, very fraught... very upset.
Judy:	Where's my sister? She is alright isn't she? Come on... where is she?
Davis:	Well we're not quite sure. We're doing our best to get in contact with your mum. Now you're going to have to put on a hospital gown. The doctor wants to examine you to see if you're injured at all. I'll leave you here for a moment so that you can get changed. You do sometimes feel aggressive to drunk drivers. I thought... you silly girl... how could you have done this? Didn't you realise what could happen? You deliberately chose to drive. She just didn't consider that she could end up killing somebody... killing her own sister.
Judy:	I want to see Joanna. That's all I want to do. Why wont you let me?
Davis:	You'll have to see the traffic police first. They should be here in a minute.
Judy:	What are they going to do?
Davis:	Well you know... if they do charge you, you'll have to face up to it, but there again it's not the end of the world. People do get done for bad driving; they pay their fine and that's the end of it. Fortunately that night casualty wasn't that busy so I was able to sit with her for a considerable time... it seemed like a lifetime actually. I talked to her about her baby... I'd just become a Granny. I was using delaying tactics to stop her from getting too close to the fact that her sister had actually been killed. I didn't want to give her the chance to ask me what was happening. I think she probably knew, but just didn't dare ask... she didn't want to hear the answer... yes, she must have realised we were stalling.

Judy:	I was ever so confused. It was like... like being in a ball of cotton wool and trying to get out and make sense of everything and I couldn't... The main thing I wanted to know was that Joanna was Ok. I was, so I thought she'd only have a couple of scratches. I mean... it was only a short journey and from where I was stood the car didn't look too bad. There were no other cars involved... I just didn't think it could have been that serious.
Davis:	It looks as though the traffic police have arrived. They'll want to breathalyse you.
Judy:	So long as you'll let me see my sister!
Davis:	They breathalysed her. It was positive. 184 milligrams. Over two times the legal limit.
Judy:	Right! Now can I see Jo?
Davis:	I'll let you go in a minute... I promise you.
Judy:	You knew I wanted to see her! That's why I co-operated! I'm getting out of this stupid bloody thing to look for her on my own.
Davis:	*(Restraining Judy)* You have to stay here! We can't have patients walking around the hospital. I'm sorry but you'll have to wait.
Judy:	She must have thought I was a maniac! I remember being stuck in this poxy hospital when I really wanted to go home. I hated it there... I hate hospitals anyway... I hate being ill and they all seemed to think something was wrong with me. I didn't have any aches or pains or nothing... well ... some cuts on my knuckles... little diddy cuts where all the glass had smashed in... but I saw no reason to stay there!
Davis:	I remember Mum arriving. It was very tense... very fraught.
P.C. Caten:	*(To Vi.)* This is Sister *(or, Charge Nurse)* Davis.
Davis:	I've been looking after Judy.

P.C. Caten:	Perhaps it would be a good idea for you to go and have a cup of tea with Sister *(or, Charge Nurse)* Davis while I explain the whole situation to Judy.
Davis:	Would you like to come this way Mrs. Poulton?
P.C. Caten:	Judy. *(Judy turns the wheelchair to face him.)*
Judy:	Please Chris... please tell me what's going on... why are they keeping me here?
P.C. Caten:	I want you to be really brave.
Judy:	Why? What's wrong? What are they going to do to me?
P.C. Caten:	Promise me you're going to be really brave.
Judy:	Just tell me what's wrong!
P.C. Caten:	Judy... Joanna died in the accident.
	(Silence)
Judy:	You're lying. What a horrible thing to say! How can anybody say that to someone?
P.C. Caten:	I'm really, really sorry. I know it's a horrible thing to say but it is true. Jo did die in the accident.
Judy:	I don't believe it! You must be lying! I'm not hurt... so why is Jo?
P.C. Caten:	Judy... I'm not lying to you. You know me better than that.
Judy:	I don't believe you. Let me see her.. then I'll believe you.
P.C. Caten:	No... you won't want to see her.
Judy:	Why? Was it really horrible? *(Silence)* Just tell me what's happened to her.
P.C. Caten:	It doesn't matter now Judy.
Judy:	No. Not my sister... not my beautiful sister. Why the hell did I do it? *(Pause)* What will Mum say?
P.C. Caten:	I've already seen your mum.

Judy:	What did she say? Is she here? I don't want to see her... I can't!
P.C. Caten:	She's not blaming you. She's very concerned about you.
Judy:	You've told her about Jo?
P.C. Caten:	Yes. *(Pause)* She's obviously very upset and she's going to need your support very much.
Judy:	Where is she?
P.C. Caten:	She's with Sister *(or, Charge Nurse)* Davis... having a cup of tea.
Judy:	She's here!
P.C. Caten:	Yes.
Judy:	No!
P.C. Caten:	Now listen... listen to me carefully. *(Pause)* Your mum is not blaming you for the accident. She's not going to come in here and have a go at you. She is very concerned about you? Do you understand what I'm saying Judy?
Judy:	Yes.
P.C. Caten:	You've both lost someone very close to you... and you're both very upset.
Davis:	I was a bit apprehensive about how Mum would react. I half wondered if she might go in there and belt the life out of Judy. I was thinking how I would react in the same situation... I could identify with her in that I'd got two daughters about the same age. I was quite fraught about the whole thing.
P.C. Caten:	Judy's ready to see you Vi. Now don't forget what I said... you're going to have to put on a brave face regardless of how much it hurts, otherwise Judy's going to blame herself for Jo's death... it's clearly very important that she doesn't do that. Sister *(or Charge Nurse)* Davis will show you the way. Vi... go and comfort her.

Davis:	Are you going to be Ok?
Vi:	Yes... don't worry. *(Silence)* There were curtains in front of each cubicle. Judy was in the fourth cubicle. She was sitting in a wheelchair. She was obviously shocked. She was I suppose... like a zombie... just couldn't relate to anything. She was... like... white as a sheet and just kept looking... staring at me. I felt she was waiting for me to have a go at her... which was the last thing in the world I was going to do. *(They embrace.)*
Judy:	I just can't stand it. I'll never be able to live again!
Vi:	Come on kid. We'll get you home.
Judy:	Mum. I wouldn't have driven if it hadn't been... I'm not supposed to tell you... but she... I only drove because Jo'd already been convicted. I wasn't meant to tell you... she made me promise not to tell you. She didn't want you to worry. I'm really, really sorry Mum!
Vi:	It was an accident. Come on. Chris has got his car. He's going to get us home.
Judy:	There was an instant of panic when I had to get into the car. I sort of backed off and thought "Oh no!", but I just sort of got into the car.
Vi:	When we got home I sat her down by the fire... just Judy and me... and I said: "No way in the world do I blame you. I love you very, very much. I need you as much as you need me. I desperately need you to help me. You've got to help me Judy. I'll help you but you've got to help your mum, Judy. I'll help you... but you've got to help me through this too." Then we just drifted into talking about ordinary things.

Judy: I remember thinking that the next morning it would turn out to have been a nightmare. I'd be at home in my bed and I'd think... "what a horrible nightmare that was." But it wasn't... obviously... I was just in a kind of daze.
I kept thinking the phone was going to ring and it's going to be Joanna, and she's going to say "Ha ha this was a joke", – and I'd think... "Oh what a sick joke!"... I used to think that there'd be a knock at the door and things like that.
You think of anything except facing the truth of what's happened. I thought that for about six months... I just couldn't accept it.
I had a nightmare not long ago about it. All I can remember is that I turned round and saw Joanna sitting in the car... really horrible... munched up and she turned to me and said ..
"Look what you've done to my face!". That really freaked me out, because for the first time it made me wonder... would she have forgiven me if she had survived. Well, would you?
Needless to say, I didn't sleep at all for the rest of that night. When I got my clothes back they were, like... smothered in big globs of blood... it was horrible... I wasn't expecting it and I had to have it cleaned. Do you know... I hadn't talked to anyone about the accident before Mark Wheeller interviewed me for this play three years after it happened. Chris Caten had said it might do some good... so that's why I did it. Without this I'd've probably never talked about it. I still think about it every day. It may just be a one second thought through my mind... like ... "Why did I ever do that?", but I did... didn't I? And that's all there is to it.
If I had one wish in the whole world, it'd be to go back to that night and....

Judy & Jo: Two sisters from Essex... out on the town.

Jo: Decked out with button open and hint of bra,

Judy: Zipped in tight...

Jo & Judy:	... tramped up we are... up... up... and away... to the local Wine bar.
	(Bob & Nob Enter.)
Judy, Jo, Bob & Nob:	Cue! Blokes in the Wine Bar.
Bob:	Looking good with slicked back hair.
Nob:	Feeling "cool"... no underwear!
Bob:	With throbbing – can't get enough of it – body tone.
Nob:	That's why they call us...
Bob & Nob:	*(Pause)* "Testosterone"
Bob:	*(Seeing Jo & Judy.)* Nob... Look!
Bob & Nob:	Whoo!... Tasty!... Essex girls!!!
Nob:	Get 'em drinking.
Bob:	Stop 'em thinking.
Nob:	Give it some rabbit.
Bob & Nob:	In for the kill and they grab it!
Judy & Jo:	Like two warriors they approach us...
Jo:	... that one's mine!
Judy:	"Good luck to you", I reply, as I hear...
Judy & Jo:	... their crappy chat up line.
Bob & Nob:	*(Adopting clinched poses.)* Hello gorgeous... and what's a nice girl like you doing in a place like this?
Judy & Jo:	Avoiding plonkers like you!
Bob:	How can they resist us?
Nob:	With this piece de resistance...
Bob & Nob:	Hey... look at you two with your curves... and us... us with no brakes.

Judy & Jo:	Flattery'll get you everywhere!
Nob:	Just what we hoped!
Bob & Nob:	Darlin'... d'ya wanna drink?
Jo:	Judy. What do you think?
Judy:	I think they're plonkers! *(They laugh hysterically.)*
Judy & Jo:	*(Suddenly deadly serious)* But mines a white wine...
Judy:	A bottle of white wine!
Jo:	Each!
Judy:	No strings attached.
All:	Drink!
Bob:	Drink!
Judy:	Drink!
Nob:	Drink!
Jo:	Drink!
Jo & Judy: **Bob & Nob:**	Brahms and Liszt we're totally pissed. *(General merriment... perhaps a rowdy [rugby?] song.)*
Jo:	A bottle of wine and I'm still standing! *(Laughter)* Come on Judy we'd better get out before we're thrown out.
Judy:	You're not going to drive home in that state are you Jo?
Jo:	I'm alright... don't worry about me!
Judy:	Why don't we catch a cab? It'll only be a couple of quid. I'll bring you back here to pick the car up tomorrow afternoon.
Jo:	You're like our mum you are... worry, worry, worry.
Judy:	Come on Jo... I'll pay.
Jo:	Oh alright then... anything to keep you quiet.

Judy: You go and phone... I'll go and get your stuff from the car... can I have the keys?

(Jo throws the keys to Judy. She catches them. Jo exits. Judy is alone on stage. Slowly she turns to the audience.)

But I can't ever go back to that night... I realise that ... so... resigned... I think that's the word... I'm resigned to the fact that it's happened.

There's no way that I'm suddenly a pure white character with no faults. It hasn't put me off drink. I still have a glass of wine, or half a lager... but I will never drink and drive again as long as I live... never ever... I just couldn't do it.

Please feel free to edit sensitively where necessary.

Judy:

The accident happened on the 20th May 1983. Resigned... I think that's the word. I'm resigned to the fact that it has happened.

If you go through life with a big guilt complex afterwards, you just end up hurting everybody else as well as yourself, 'cos you get bitter and wound up. Nothing I can do is going to change it, ever. I wouldn't have harmed Joanna, my sister, not on purpose, so I don't feel guilty about killing her... because it was... an accident.

You get so sure of yourself, so clever, well, not clever... you just don't think, 'cos you do it all the time. It only takes one person to point it out to you and you might not do it.

Before it happens you think... "Oh, I won't get caught!" I would probably never have got stopped and breathalysed. I'm having to pay for my mistake in a different way.

I still think about it every day. It may just be a one second thought through my mind... like... **"Why** did I ever do that?", but I did... didn't I? **And** that's all there is to it.

At first I kept thinking the phone was going to ring and it's going to be Joanna, and she's going to say "Ha ha this was a joke", – and I'd think..."Oh what a sick joke!"... I used to think that there'd be a knock at the door and things like that. You think of anything except facing the truth of what's happened. I thought that for about six months... I just couldn't accept it.

I remember thinking that the next morning it would turn out to have been a nightmare. I'd be at home in my bed and I'd think... "what a horrible nightmare that was." But it wasn't... obviously... I was just in a kind of daze.

I actually did have a nightmare not long ago about it. All I can remember is that I turned round and saw Joanna sitting in the car... really horrible... munched up and she turned to me and said... "Look what you've done to my face!" That really freaked me out, because for the first time it made me wonder... would she have forgiven me if she had survived.

Well, would you?

Needless to say, I didn't sleep at all for the rest of that night. When I got my clothes back they were, like... smothered in big globs of blood... it was horrible... wasn't expecting it... I had to have it cleaned.

I hadn't talked to anyone about the accident before Mark Wheeller interviewed me for this play... three years after Jo's death. Chris Caten said it might do some good... so that's why I did it. Without this I'd've probably never talked about it.

If I had one wish in the whole world, it'd be to go back to that night and... but I can't... I realise that... so... resigned... I think that's the word... I'm resigned to the fact that it's happened.

There's no way that I'm suddenly a pure white character with no faults. It hasn't put me off drink. I still have a glass of wine, or half a lager... but I will never drink and drive again as long as I live... never ever... I just couldn't do it.

THE FACTS ABOUT DRINKING AND DRIVING

- Drinking and driving is the cause of many deaths and injuries, each year.

- There is no sure way to know how much you can drink and still be under the legal limit – it depends on your weight, sex, age and metabolism, as well as on the type of drink you are having.

- Alcohol is absorbed fast by the body but it goes away slowly. There is nothing you can do (black coffee, cold showers, etc.) to get rid of alcohol faster – it just takes its time.

- It is quite possible to be above the legal alcohol limit in the morning if you have been drinking the night before.

- The only safe way is **NOT TO DRINK AT ALL** if you are driving.

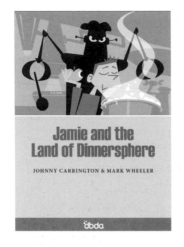

Jamie and the Land of Dinnersphere

JOHNNY CARRINGTON & MARK WHEELER

öbda

ISBN 978 1 902843 25 4

Cast: 2m and 2f with doubling or 3m, 1f and 5 or 6m/f. Suitable for use as a TIE production in the new vocational courses for ages 13+ (or as a performance piece in Primary schools)
Duration: 35 minutes (55 minutes with the workshop)

SCH**OO**L F**OO**D TRUST
Eat Better Do Better

NEW! – JAMIE AND THE LAND OF DINNERSPHERE
(a Healthy school dinners play) by Johnny Carrington & Mark Wheeller

Jamie Jamjar loves healthy food. He has seen how a poor diet can mess you up… just by looking at his sister… Lazy Lillian! Jamie is shocked when his school tries out the new Robot Dudes (fast food servants) who replace the friendly dinner ladies. Jamie then discovers his own father invented them!

Can it get any worse? Yes it can!

Jamie is transported to Dinnersphere (in another of his father's inventions, a Story Rocket) where Jamie discovers the nefarious Dinnerwitch, busy planning world domination through putrid school dinners! Together with three friends, Bo, Agor and another - a member of the Primary School audience - they confront and defeat the Dinnerwitch!

Jamie provides an opportunity for secondary school students to present an interactive Theatre In Education play with all the joys of the audience being a key part of the final performance. It is expected to become a staple part of the new vocational courses where there are, at the moment, few plays which will fit the specification so well!

The text includes an innovative interactive workshop written by Adrian New (Stopwatch Theatre) which can be led by the secondary students.

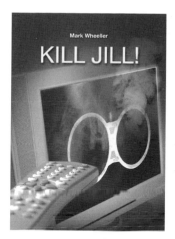

Mark Wheeller

KILL JILL!

ISBN 978 1 902843 20 9

Cast: 11+ (3m, 3f & 5 m or f)
Suitable for GCSE with doubling
(2m, 2f & 1 m or f)
Duration: 50 minutes approx.
Suitable for: ages 13+
or adults!

Commissioned and
premiered by The
Birmingham Rep Theatre

NEW! – KILL JILL
by Mark Wheeller

Big Brother meets Kill Bill meets Jack
(of Beanstalk fame) meets Tony Martin...
Mix these together to create *Kill Jill!*
This brand new play by Mark Wheeller
explores the topical issues of homeowners
defending themselves, and asks "How far
can Reality TV be allowed to go?"

Jill is the latest victim of Reality Lottery,
a futuristic form of National Service to
entertainment. She accompanies Jack as
he (again) robs George, who lies in wait
armed with a shotgun. The Reality Lottery
camera operators are filming everything...
but should they intervene? The ending is
suitably Tarantinoesque!

Kill Jill! raises issues of rights and
responsibilities. It is a play full of
interesting techniques that will delight
Drama teachers and students, and will
thrill those exploring Citizenship issues
through imaginative and entertaining
Theatre productions.

'Kill Jill is a very fizzy ride! What a great
script! The playfulness with style and
wide range of reference points with an
'anytime, anyplace, anywhere' theatrical
freedom... the banter goes to some
strange places too - perhaps a Python
influence? The build up of tension in the
visit to George's castle puts the end of the
play in firm thriller territory! Wonderful
stuff!!!!!'

*Paul Mills, Head of Drama,
Westgate School, Winchester*

ISBN 978 1 902843 26 1

Cast: 6 (3m, 3f with doubling). Can be performed with a cast of up to around 30. (10m, 8f & 12 m or f)
Duration: 55 minutes
Suitable for: ages 13+ or adults!

Developed from Mark Wheeller's stage play Race To Be Seen, written with the Epping Youth Theatre.

Available on DVD, the award winning Oaklands Youth Theatre production. *For more information contact dbda.*

Graham - World's Fastest Blind Runner!

Written in the same documentary style as Too Much Punch For Judy, Mark's first version of this play about Graham Salmon MBE, was awarded Critics Choice at the Edinburgh Festival Fringe (1984).

It has recently been re-written, and on it's first two outings won through to the Final of both the National Drama Festivals Association in 2007 and the All England Theatre Festival in 2008, winning different awards at each Festival.

Listed in the Guinness Book of Records as The World's Fastest Blind Runner in 1976 (100m in 11.4 secs) Graham went on to play Golf for the international visually impaired team for whom he hit a famous "hole in one" in The British Open!

"I didn't ever need convincing that 'Graham' was an ideal piece to challenge my group and that it ticked all the boxes for A-level work, but if I ever needed justification, then the results have certainly given it. In the breakdown of the Unit 2 marks i.e. the performance of 'Graham', all seven candidates were awarded 100%. It's worth noting that the external moderator was accompanied that evening by her senior examiner! Thanks again for the material and thanks to Graham, such an inspirational person!"
Mike Fleetwood, Parkside Arts College.

ISBN 978-1-902843-33-9

Cast: (3m, 5f, 4m or f)
Duration: 60 minutes approx.
Suitable for: **KS 4/5+**

CHEQUERED FLAGS TO CHEQUERED FUTURES
by Mark Wheeller

Chequered Flags to Chequered Futures is Mark Wheeller's latest verbatim play. It tells the true story of Chris Gilfoy, the Rookies World Champion Banger Racer in 2000.

When he was thirteen he worked with Mark Wheeller as a central part of the development team for Chicken. The main character in that play was named after him. Towards the end of that play "Chris" says: People would say I'd encouraged her with a dare They'd make judgements and suspect I didn't care They'd say I should have known better... should have been more mature. But everyone knows... for a moments stupidity there is no known cure.

These lines would haunt Chris in his real life. In 2006 Chris was being driven along a public road in a powerful BMW by a racing friend. She was thought to be driving at 90 mph in a 30 limit. They crashed into a wall. None were wearing seatbelts and, unknown to Chris, the driver was uninsured. The consequences for all three in the car were life changing. The play tells the fast paced story through the words of Chris and his family. In a parallel strand of powerful monologues Jane, the mother of the driver, tells her story of the aftermarth of the accident.

Mark says this will be his final road traffic accident play. It is, he believes, his best! The play was premiered by students from the Victoria Shanghai Academy in Hong Kong in October 2014, where it was presented with OYT's new version of Chicken.

Ideal for TIE, One Act Play competitions and as a KS4/5 (and beyond) course book.

Other plays published by **Ten Alps Communicate**

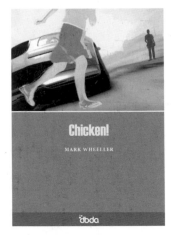

ISBN 978 1 902843 19 3

Cast: 34m, 3f & 2m/f or 2m & 2f for GCSE
Duration: 35 minutes approx.
KS 3 & 4.

CHICKEN! by Mark Wheeller
New Updated Edition

A 'new and improved' version of WHY DID THE CHICKEN CROSS THE ROAD? The play tells the story of two cousins, Tammy and Chris. We are led to believe that something bad will happen to Chris who refuses to wear his cycle helmet. It is, however, Tammy who gets killed on the one morning that the cousins walk to school. Chris remains unwilling to tell anyone of his part in the accident and he has to live with this dreadful secret. One of the main changes is the introduction of Chris filming Tammy's fatal dare on his mobile phone camera.

'We have just been fortunate enough to witness the most superb exhibition of interactive safety education. The performance was quite stunning!'

Jim Lambert, Head Teacher Sinclair Middle School, Southampton

---

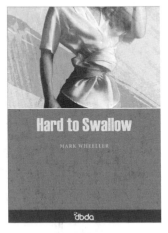

ISBN 978 1 902843 08 7

Cast: 3f & 2m with doubling, or 6f, 3m & 16
Duration: 70 minutes approx.
KS 3 to adult

Hard to Swallow by Mark Wheeller

This play is an adaptation of Maureen Dunbar's award winning book (and film) **Catherine** which charts her daughter's uneven battle with anorexia and the family's difficulties in coping with the illness.

The play has gone on to be performed all over the world to much acclaim, achieving considerable success in One Act Play Festivals. Its simple narrative style means that it is equally suitable for adult and older youth groups to perform.

'This play reaches moments of almost unbearable intensity... naturalistic scenes flow seamlessly into sequences of highly stylised theatre... such potent theatre!'
Vera Lustiq, The Independent

'Uncompromising and sensitive... should be compulsory viewing to anyone connected with the education of teenagers.'

Mick Martin, Times Educational Supplement